TRAV
THEA

Traverse Theatre Company

Any Given Day

By Linda McLean

Cast

Sadie	Kathryn Howden
Bill	Lewis Howden
Jackie	Kate Dickie
Dave	Phil McKee
Boy	Jamie Quinn

Director	Dominic Hill
Designer	Jonathan Fensom
Lighting Designer	Lizzie Powell
Sound Designer	John Harris

Assistant Director	Ant Stones
Company Stage Manager	Gemma Smith
Deputy Stage Managers	Dan Dixon
	Sunita Hinduja
Wardrobe Supervisor	Sarah Holland
Fight Director	Raymond Short

First performed at the Traverse Theatre
Saturday 29 May 2010

A Traverse Theatre Commission

THE TRAVERSE

Artistic Director: Dominic Hill

The Traverse has an unrivalled reputation for producing contemporary theatre of the highest quality, invention and energy, and for its dedication to new writing.
(Scotland on Sunday)

The Traverse is Scotland's New Writing Theatre. From its conception in 1963, it has embraced a spirit of innovation and risk-taking that launched the careers of many of Scotland's best-known writers including John Byrne, David Greig, David Harrower and Liz Lochhead. It is unique in Scotland in that it fulfils the crucial role of providing the infrastructure, professional support and expertise to ensure the development of a dynamic theatre culture for Scotland. It commissions and develops new plays or adaptations from contemporary playwrights, producing, on average, six Traverse Theatre Company productions or co-productions per year. It also presents a large number of productions from visiting companies from across the UK. These include new plays, adaptations, dance, physical theatre, puppetry and contemporary music. As well as the August Festival, it is the home of the Manipulate Visual Theatre Festival, the Bank of Scotland Imaginate Festival and the Traverse's own autumn Festival.

The Traverse Theatre, the festival's most prestigious home of serious drama. (New York Times)

The Traverse is a pivotal venue in Edinburgh and this is particularly the case during the Edinburgh Festival – positioned as it is between the Edinburgh Festival Fringe and the Edinburgh International Festival. The Traverse programme overall won twenty-two awards in 2009.

A Rolls-Royce machine for promoting new Scottish drama across Europe and beyond. (The Scotsman)

The Traverse's work with young people is of major importance and takes the form of encouraging playwriting through its flagship education project, Class Act, as well as the Young Writers' Group. Class Act is now in its twentieth year and gives school pupils the opportunity to develop their plays with professional playwrights and work with directors and actors to see the finished pieces performed on stage at the Traverse. The hugely successful Young Writers' Group is open to new writers aged 18 – 25. A new project, Scribble, offers an after-school playwriting and theatre skills workshop for 14 – 17 year olds. Both programmes are led by professional playwrights. The Traverse is now in its second year working with young men from Scottish prisons to improve their literacy and oracy skills through practical drama and playwriting in a project called Open Write. The participants work with theatre professionals to develop their own plays which are performed at the Traverse.

Traverse Theatre, Scotland's New Writing Theatre
10 Cambridge Street, Edinburgh EH1 2ED

CHARITY NO. SC002368

COMPANY BIOGRAPHIES

Kate Dickie (*Jackie*)

An award-winning stage and film actress, Kate trained at RSAMD. Her feature-film debut was *Red Road* for which she received the British Independent Film Award for Best Actress, the Best Actress Award at the Festival du Nouveau Cinéma, Montréal, and the BAFTA (Scotland) Best Actress Award. Kate's work for the Traverse: *What We Know* (co-produced with Ek performance). Other theatre work includes: *Aalst* (National Theatre of Scotland); *Trojan Women* (Cryptic Theatre); *Running Girl* (Boilerhouse); *The Entertainer* (Citizens Theatre). Film work includes: *Outcast, Shelter, Wasted* (Raindog Films); *Somers Town*, directed by Shane Meadows; *Summer*, directed by Kenneth Glennan and the forthcoming *Rounding Up Donkeys,* directed by Morag MacKinnon. Television work includes: *Five Daughters, Tinsel Town, Garrows Law* (BBC); *He Kills Coppers* (Ecosse); *The Vice* (Carlton); and the forthcoming *The Pillars of the Earth* (Tandem) and *Dive* (ITV).

Jonathan Fensom (Designer)

Jonathan's work for the Traverse: Edward Albee's *The Goat, or Who is Sylvia?* Other theatre work includes: *King Lear, Love's Labour's Lost* (Shakespeare's Globe); *Swan Lake* (San Francisco Ballet); *Journey's End* (West End, Broadway; Tony Award nomination for Best Scenic Design, 2007); *The American Plan, Pygmalion* (New York); *The Homecoming, Big White Fog* (Almeida Theatre); *Happy Now?, The Mentalists, Burn, Citizenship, Chatroom* (Royal National Theatre); *In the Club, born bad, In Arabia We'd All Be Kings, Abigail's Party, What the Butler Saw* (Hampstead Theatre); *Duck, Talking to Terrorists, The Sugar Syndrome* (Royal Court); *Kindertransport, Breakfast with Emma* (Shared Experience); *The Tempest* (Tron Theatre); *Crown Matrimonial* (Guildford, tour); *The Faith Healer* (The Gate, Dublin/Broadway); *God of Hell* (Donmar Warehouse); *National Anthems* (Old Vic); *M.A.D., Little Baby Nothing* (Bush Theatre); *Be My Baby* (Soho Theatre); *Candide, Charley's Aunt* (Oxford Playhouse); *Small Family Business, Little Shop of Horrors* (West Yorkshire Playhouse); *My Night With Reg, Dealer's Choice* (Birmingham Rep); *After the Dance, Hay Fever* (Oxford Stage Company); *So Long Life* (Theatre Royal Bath) and *Wozzeck* (Birmingham Opera and European tour). Jonathan was Associate Designer on Disney's *The Lion King*, which premiered at the New Amsterdam Theatre on Broadway and has subsequently opened worldwide.

John Harris (Sound Designer)

John was, for several years, assistant organist at St Giles' Cathedral, Edinburgh, and took his Masters degree in composition at the RSAMD in Glasgow. He also writes concert music and directs the Red Note Ensemble. John's work for the Traverse: *The Dark Things,The Last Witch* (co-produced with Edinburgh International Festival); *Lucky Box, Nobody Will Ever Forgive Us, Nasty, Brutish and Short, The Dogstone* (co-produced with Òran Mór); *The Nest, Knives in Hens, Anna Weiss, Family, Perfect Days, Greta, Sharp Shorts, Kill the Old, Torture Their Young.* Other theatre work includes: *Monaciello* (Tron/Naples International Theatre Festival); *Julie, Mary Queen of Scots, Gobbo* (National Theatre of Scotland); *Mother Courage, Jack and the Beanstalk* (Dundee Rep); *Jerusalem* (West Yorkshire Playhouse); *Midwinter, Solstice* (Royal Shakespeare Company). Opera includes: *Death of a Scientist* (Scottish Opera 5:15 series); *Sleep, Sleep/What is She?/The Sermon* (Tapestry Opera Theatre, Toronto). Film and television work includes: *The Fingertrap* (BAFTA Scotland Emerging Talent Award, 2009); *Saltmark* (Blindside); *The Emperor, The Green Man of Knowledge* (Red Kite).

Dominic Hill (Director)

Dominic became Artistic Director of the Traverse Theatre in January 2008. Before joining the Traverse, he was Artistic Director of Dundee Rep Theatre from 2003–2007. Work for the Traverse: Edward Albee's *The Goat, or Who is Sylvia?, The Dark Things, The Last Witch* (co-produced with the Edinburgh International Festival), *Heaven* by Simon Stephens, *Kyoto* by David Greig, *Lucky Box* by David Harrower (co-produced with Òran Mór), *The Dogstone* by Kenny Lindsay, *Nasty, Brutish and Short* by Andy Duffy (both co-produced with the National Theatre of Scotland), *Fall* by Zinnie Harris. Productions for Dundee Rep Theatre include: *Peer Gynt* (co-produced with the National Theatre of Scotland, winner of Best Director and Best Production, Critics' Awards for Theatre in Scotland 2008), *Happy Days, Hansel and Gretel, A Midsummer Night's Dream, Monkey, The Talented Mr Ripley, Ubu the King, The Graduate, Macbeth, Scenes from an Execution* (winner of Best Director and Best Production, Critics' Awards for Theatre in Scotland 2003), *Peter Pan, Twelfth Night, Dancing at Lughnasa, The Snow Queen, The Duchess of Malfi, The Winter's Tale* (nominated for Best Director, Barclays/TMA Awards). For Scottish Opera: *Falstaff, Macbeth.* For the Young Vic: *A Prayer for My Daughter.*

Kathryn Howden (*Sadie*)

Kathryn's work for the Traverse: *The Last Witch* (co-produced with Edinburgh International Festival), *The Ballad of Crazy Paola, Abandonment, Passing Places, Poor Superman* (co-produced with Hampstead Theatre), *Bondagers, The Hope Slide, Buchanan.* Other theatre work includes: *Every One* (Royal Lyceum, Edinburgh); *That Face* (Tron); *Be Near Me* (National Theatre of Scotland/Donmar Warehouse); *Trumpets and Raspberries, All My Sons, Six Black Candles, The Breathing House, Victory, A View from the Bridge, The Taming of the Shrew, A Family Affair, The Marriage of Figaro* (Royal Lyceum Theatre, Edinburgh); *Phaedre* (Perth Theatre); *Gilt, Road, Nae Problem* (7:84 Theatre

Company); *Vipers Opium, Earthquake Weather, Never-Before-Seen Familiar* (Starving Artists Theatre Company, USA); *Shooting Ducks, Just Frank* (Theatre Royal, Stratford East); *Swing Hammer Swing!* (Citizens Theatre); *The Government Inspector* (Almeida Theatre). Television work includes: *Dear Green Place, Rockface, Looking after Jo Jo, Taggart, Night and Day, Peak Practice, Big Cat, Around Scotland, Macrame Man, Let Yourself Go, New Year Pieces.* Film work includes: *The 39 Steps, The Pen, Karmic Mothers, The Priest and the Pirate.*

Lewis Howden (*Bill*)
Lewis trained at RSAMD. Work for the Traverse: *Petrol Jesus Nightmare #5 (In the Time of the Messiah), The Nest, Olga, Knives in Hens, The House Among the Stars, Loose Ends.* Other theatre work includes: *Confessions of a Justified Sinner, Tartuffe, Merlin the Magnificent, Mother Courage, Cuttin' a Rug* (Royal Lyceum Theatre, Edinburgh); *Defender of the Faith, The Beauty Queen of Leenane, The Trick is to Keep Breathing* (Tron Theatre); *Caged Heat, The Big Funk, The Crucible, Glengarry Glen Ross* (Arches); *No Mean City, Nightingale, Chase* (Citizens Theatre); *Macbeth, Educating Agnes, Medea, King Lear* (Theatre Babel); *Mary Queen of Scots Got Her Head Chopped Off, Our Teacher's a Troll* (National Theatre of Scotland); *Riddance* (Paines Plough); *Word for Word* (Magnetic North); *Fire in the Basement* (Communicado); *Broken Glass, Frankie and Johnny* (Rapture); *The Angel's Share* (Borderline); *The Algebra of Freedom* (7:84 Theatre Company); *Quelques Fleurs, Tartuffe* (Nippy Sweeties). Lewis has also been heard in many radio plays. Film and television work includes: *Taggart, Rebus, Monarch of the Glen, Dr Findlay, Hope Springs, Strathblair, Turning World, The Chief, Aberdeen, The Blue Boy, Slide.*

Phil McKee (*Dave*)
Theatre work includes: *That Face* (Tron Theatre); *Relocated* (Royal Court); *Noughts & Crosses* (RSC); *Mary Stuart* (National Theatre of Scotland); *Julius Caesar* (Royal Lyceum Theatre, Edinburgh); *Damages, Stitching* (Bush Theatre); *8000 M* (Suspect Culture); *Richard III, Napoli Milonaria* (Royal National Theatre). Film work includes: *Clash of the Titans* (Warner Bros.); *Joan of Arc* (Gaumont); *The Lost Battalion* (A&E); *The Debt Collector* (Channel Four Films); *George and the Dragon* (Apollo Media); *The Shepherd* (Sony Pictures); *Beginner's Luck* (Angel Film & Television). Television work includes: *Band of Brothers* (HBO); *Ghost Squad* (Channel 4); *The Family* (ITV); *Taggart, Heartbeat, Soldier Soldier* (ITV); *Silent Witness, Lost in France, Crime Traveller* (BBC); *Richard II* (Illuminations).

Linda McLean (*Writer*)
Linda McLean was born in Glasgow where she studied at Strathclyde University and Jordanhill College of Education. She travelled as a teacher in Europe, America, Africa and Scandinavia before she wrote plays. Her

plays for the Traverse include: *strangers, babies* (Susan Smith Blackburn Prize finalist), *Shimmer* (Herald Angel), *Olga* (from the original Finnish play by Laura Ruohonen) and *One Good Beating* (winner of Best One Act Play, 2008). Other work includes: *Riddance* (Paines Plough, Fringe First and Herald Angel Awards); *Cold Cuts, Doch an Doris* (7:84 Theatre Company); *Word for Word* (Magnetic North); *Reminded of Beauty* (RSAMD); *Like Water for Chocolate* (Théâtres sans Frontières, from the novel by Laura Esquivel). Radio work includes: *And So Say All of Us* (BBC Radio 3, co-written with Duncan McMillan and Dan Rebellato). Linda is Chairwoman of the Playwrights' Studio Scotland and has worked for the British Council in Mexico City, Teluca, Oslo and Bogota. She regularly works in schools and colleges, encouraging new writers to find their own voices. In 2009 she delivered the keynote speech to the Playwrights' Guild of Canada. Linda is currently under commission to the Traverse Theatre, National Theatre of Scotland and Magnetic North. *Riddance* is currently playing in Athens and *strangers, babies* has been selected by Théâtre Ouvert in Paris as part of their Playwrights in Partnership exchange. In October 2010 Linda will take up the IASH Edinburgh University/Traverse creative fellowship.

Lizzie Powell (Lighting Designer)

Lizzie trained at LAMDA. Her lighting work for the Traverse includes: *The Dark Things*, the Debuts season and *Rupture* (co-produced with National Theatre of Scotland). Other theatre work includes: *Huxley's Lab* (Grid Iron); *Treasure Island* (Wee Stories); *Transform Glasgow, Transform Orkney, Mary Queen of Scots Got Her Head Chopped Off, Our Teacher's a Troll, Rupture, Venus as a Boy, The Recovery Position* (National Theatre of Scotland); *First You're Born* (Plutôt la Vie); *Pobby & Dingan, The Book of Beasts* (Catherine Wheels); *Under Milk Wood* (Theatre Royal, Northampton); *The Death of Harry, Making History* (Ouroborous Productions, Dublin); *The Wasp Factory*, (Cumbernauld Theatre); *The Wall* (Borderline Theatre); *Second City Trilogy* (Cork Opera House); *Smallone, Romeo and Juliet, This Ebony Bird, Tricky* (Blood In The Alley Productions); *Drenched* (Boiler House Productions); *The Night Shift* (Fuel Productions). Lizzie was assistant to the Lighting Designer on *Billy Elliot* at the Victoria Palace Theatre, London.

Jamie Quinn (*Boy*)

Jamie trained at the Drama Centre, London. *Any Given Day* marks Jamie's professional theatre debut. His television work includes: *Still Game* (BBC/Comedy Unit); *Taggart* (SMG); *Butterfingers* (CITV); *High Times* (SMG); *River City* (BBC Scotland). His film work includes: *Parliamo Glasgow* (IWC Media/Ch 4); *Wild Country* (Gabriel Films); *At the End of the Sentence, Wiseguys* (BBC Scotland/Tartan Short); *Lord of the Fleas* (Tern Television).

SPONSORSHIP AND DEVELOPMENT

We would like to thank the following
corporate sponsors for their recent support

New Arts Sponsorship Grants
Supported by the Scottish Government
In conjunction with
A&B
Arts & Business Scotland

  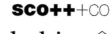

To find out how you can benefit from being a Traverse Corporate
Sponsor, please contact Fiona Sturgeon Shea,
Head of Communications, on 0131 228 3223 or
fiona.sturgeonshea@traverse.co.uk

The Traverse Theatre's work
would not be possible without the support of

Emerging Playwright on Attachment post supported by
Playwrights' Studio, Scotland as a Partnership Project

Pearson Playwright supported by **Pearson**

For their continued generous support of Traverse
productions, the Traverse thanks:

Habitat
Camerabase
Paterson SA Hairdressing
Stems Florist

For their help on *Any Given Day* the company would
like to thank

Pine Lodge Auction, Capitol Cooling, Edinburgh Council,
Roseleaf Bar Cafe, Lyceum Theatre Bar

TRAVERSE THEATRE – THE COMPANY

ANY GIVEN DAY

Linda McLean

For Kenneth

Characters

Play One

BILL, *fifties*
SADIE, *forties*
BOY

Play Two

JACKIE, *forties*
DAVE, *fifties*

The first play takes place in a flat in the city.

The second play takes place in a bar.

This text went to press before the end of rehearsals and so may differ slightly from the play as performed.

PLAY ONE

BILL *and* SADIE *live with each other in a council-owned flat.*

They were, for a long time, kept in a home for the 'mentally defective' but were released into the community when their and other similar institutions were closed in the early 1990s.

SADIE	Is Jackie coming?
BILL	Aye.
SADIE	…
BILL	Aye?
SADIE	Aye. Well?
BILL	Don't act daft. You know she's coming. She said she would be here.
SADIE	I'm not daft.
BILL	Daft as a bloody brush. Basil bloody Brush.
SADIE	Don't. Don't you.
BILL	HA HA HA HA
SADIE	I don't like Basil Brush.
BILL	That's you.
SADIE	Don't.
BILL	Well.
SADIE	Well yourself.
BILL	HA HA HA HA

SADIE   I'll go out of here.

BILL   You do that.
          Basil.

SADIE   Right, you.

BILL   Put the water on while you're in there.

SADIE   I'm not making tea.

BILL   Who asked you?

SADIE   It's coming.

BILL   So's Christmas.

SADIE   Aye.
          So it is.

BILL   Do you think Jackie would like flowers?

SADIE   For her Christmas?

BILL   What else?
          Her birthday's long by.

SADIE   Aye.

BILL   What kind?

SADIE   I don't know.

BILL   That's right, Basil.

SADIE   Don't.

BILL   Or vouchers?

SADIE   Vouchers.

BILL   That's what you want.

SADIE   No.

BILL   I know what you want.

SADIE   I don't think flowers grow at Christmas.

BILL   Aye.
          They do.

SADIE   Where?

BILL   Somewhere.
           They're in the Marks and Spencer book.

SADIE   Even at Christmas?

BILL   Asda an' all.

SADIE   So they are.
           I remember now.

BILL   No you don't.

SADIE   I do.
           I'll show you.
           Where is that book?

BILL   HA HA HA HA

SADIE   Right.
           That's it.
           I'm off.

BILL   Make us a cup of tea.
           While you're in there.

SADIE   No.

BILL   How no?

SADIE   You make me mad.

BILL   Make us a cup of tea.

SADIE   Do you want a cup of tea?

BILL   When do I ever say no to a cup of tea?

SADIE   I don't know.

BILL   Never.
           That's when.
           Never say no to a cup of tea.
           That's me.

SADIE   Never say no.

BILL   Refuse only blows.

SADIE	What time is it?
BILL	Early.
SADIE	That clock doesn't tell the right time.
BILL	I'm not going by the clock.
SADIE	Not going by the clock.
BILL	I've got my watch. Dafty.
SADIE	I'm not daft.
BILL	Anyway. Nothing to worry about. It's still light.
SADIE	So it is.
BILL	Jackie wouldn't come in the dark.
SADIE	No no. She couldn't come in the dark.
BILL	Don't worry.
SADIE	We couldn't open the door in the dark.
BILL	No.
SADIE	Not once it's dark.
BILL	We did once.
SADIE	That was just that once.
BILL	Once is once.
SADIE	That bad day.
BILL	I know.
SADIE	No phone no door.
BILL	I know.
SADIE	Not after dark.
BILL	Jackie won't come after dark.

SADIE   Did she say a time?

BILL   You know what she's like.

SADIE   Butterfly brain.

BILL   That's her.

SADIE   Butterflybrain.

BILL   Come away from the window.

SADIE   Just in case.
Just in case she was in the street.

BILL   Is she?

SADIE   No.
There's Ellen but.

BILL   Is it?
Is it?

SADIE   Look.
See.
Crossing the road.

BILL   No point in waving.

SADIE   How?

BILL   She won't look up.

SADIE   She might.

BILL   It's raining.

SADIE   So?

BILL   If she looks up her face'll get wet.

SADIE   I don't like that.
Wet in my face.
Even in the shower, I don't look up.

BILL   See.
She didn't look up.

SADIE   I waved anyway.

BILL   You.

SADIE   Maybe she knows I'm here, waving.

BILL   You.

SADIE   She sometimes looks up.
            She sometimes knows.

BILL   Except when it rains.

SADIE   Still.
            I wave even if she doesn't.

BILL   Aye.

SADIE   Ellen from the
            Coffeeshop.

BILL   Have we got bread?

SADIE   What for?

            …
            Toast I remember.

BILL   Have we got bread?

SADIE   I don't know.
            I don't remember.

BILL   Jackie likes toast and cheese.
            Or ham.

SADIE   I know that.

BILL   Go and see then.

SADIE   It'll be in the cupboard.

BILL   Go and see.

SADIE   I think we've got cheese.

BILL   We've got cheese.
            And ham.
            We bought them yesterday.
            Dafty.
            HA HA HA HA

She likes that thin bread.
She doesn't like thick bread.
Cuts the crusts off thick bread.
Eat your crusts and you'll get nice curly hair.
But I've already got curly hair, she says.
We've always got bread.

SADIE   None.

BILL   You didn't look.
You were too quick.

SADIE   I did so.
There's only an outsider left.

BILL   She'll never eat an outsider.
Throw it away.
Give it to the birds.

SADIE   I like an outsider.
Toast and Dairylea.

BILL   We'll need to get bread.

SADIE   Will I get my coat?

BILL   Aye.
Get your coat.

SADIE   When will it be dark?

BILL   It's only two o'clock.

SADIE   But when will it be dark?

BILL   Hours.

SADIE   How many?

BILL   As many as going on the bus to Ayr.

SADIE   That's a long time on the bus.
I always need the bathroom.

BILL   Is there no bread in the freezer?

SADIE   I don't like to look in the freezer.

BILL	Basil.
SADIE	Don't.
BILL	You bought the freezer.
SADIE	Only because Jackie said you can keep ice cream in it.
BILL	But you won't go into the freezer to get the ice cream.
SADIE	I don't need to. You get it for me.
BILL	I don't even like ice cream.
SADIE	You're good to me.
BILL	I'll see if there's any bread.
SADIE	Are you sure?
BILL	I'm not scared of the freezer.
SADIE	I know. Lucky for me. I shouldn't eat too much ice cream, Ellen said. There's a boy. He's looking up. He doesn't care about the rain. … … He didn't wave.
BILL	There's no bread in the freeze / Who are you waving at?
SADIE	A boy.
BILL	Don't wave. Come away from the window. What did I tell you?
SADIE	I forget. I forget.

BILL   Come back here so he can't see you.

SADIE   I just forget.

BILL   Okay.

SADIE   I remember now.

BILL   Okay.

SADIE   Oh.
Oh.
I remember now.

BILL   It's okay.

SADIE   Oh oh oh oh

BILL   It's okay.

SADIE   Is he still there?

BILL   There's nobody there.

SADIE   Good.
That's good.

BILL   You.

SADIE   Anyway.
He never waved back.

BILL   …

SADIE   …

BILL   There's no bread in the freezer.

SADIE   No.
I don't put bread in the freezer.

BILL   No.

SADIE   I don't want to go out now.

BILL   I'll go.

SADIE   I don't want you to go.

BILL   We've no bread.

SADIE	Maybe Jackie won't want toast.
BILL	She always has toast.
SADIE	Maybe she won't.
BILL	When has she ever not had toast?
SADIE	I don't know.
BILL	Never. That's when.
SADIE	Cheese and ham.
BILL	That's right.
SADIE	And beetroot.
BILL	That's you that likes the beetroot.
SADIE	I do.
BILL	Jackie likes tomato sauce.
SADIE	We've got tomato sauce. I saw it. Beside the bread. The outsider.
BILL	I'll get my coat.
SADIE	In a minute.
BILL	I'll put on the anorak. With the hood.
SADIE	Can't see your face in that anorak.
BILL	It's cosy.
SADIE	It's raining.
BILL	That zip.
SADIE	Mind you don't catch your chin.
BILL	Never again. Chin in. Chin down.

SADIE   Chinny chin chin again.
          There was an old man called…
          …?
          Would you like a cup of tea?

BILL   Now?

SADIE   I put on the water.
          Like you said.

BILL   You.

SADIE   A wee cup of tea.
          Against the rain.

BILL   I don't want to leave it too late.

SADIE   Cup of tea.

BILL   Be no bread left.

SADIE   Cuppa.

BILL   Just Weight Watchers.

SADIE   Tea.

BILL   A quick one then.

SADIE   And a Penguin.

BILL   You trying to make me fat?

SADIE   No.

BILL   You want me to be as fat as you?
          Fatty.

SADIE   Don't.
          Ellen says I need to lose weight.

BILL   If I get fat as you none of us'll be able to get up
               off that chair.

SADIE   You can't get as fat as me.

BILL   How no?

SADIE   I don't know.
          I just know.

BILL   Where's my tea?

SADIE   Where's my tea.
            What did your last slave die of?

BILL   Hey you.
            Hey cheeky.

SADIE   See.
            Last slave die of.

BILL   I'll batter you.

SADIE   No you'll not.

BILL   Have we got Garibaldi biscuits?
            Garibaldi biscuits.
            Cheese.
            Ham.
            Tea.
            Milk.
            Butter.

SADIE   Flora.
            She takes Flora.

BILL   We've got Flora.

SADIE   Everything she likes.

BILL   Apart from bread.

SADIE   Apart from bread.
            I'm bringing tea.
            I'll need a table.

BILL   I'll get the table.

SADIE   Tea's up.

BILL   Tea's up.

SADIE   Tea.

BILL   Tea.

            Lovely lovely hot tea-slurping heaven.

CRRRRRRRRRAACK

Tea in air.

SADIE   Oh no oh no oh no oh no oh no oh no oh no oh no
            oh no oh no oh no oh no oh no

BILL   Shh shh shhh shh shh

SADIE   Oh no oh no oh no oh oh oh oh oh oh oh oh oh

BILL   Shoosh shoosh shoosh shoosh shoosh

SADIE   Ooooooooooooooooooooooooooooooooooooooooo

BILL   Sadie.
            Sadie.
            Sadie.

SADIE   AAAAAAAAAAAAAAAAAAAAAAAAAAAAAA

BILL   He'll hear you.
            He'll hear you.

SADIE   AAAAAAAAAAAAAAAAAAAAAAAAAAAAAAAA

BILL   Shutup.

SADIE   Shutupshutupshutupshutupshutupshutupshutup
            shutupshutup

            BILL *lies on top of* SADIE *to stop her hurting*
            herself. She struggles for a while. She stops
            struggling. She might go again, nothing's sure yet.

BILL   Good job we got those plastic mugs. Eh?

SADIE   …

BILL   Eh?

SADIE   …

BILL   Be cups and saucers to clear up as well as glass.

SADIE   …

BILL   Those plastic mugs.
            Eh?

SADIE   …

BILL   Good job.

SADIE   We got them for you.

BILL   I know.
            I know that.

SADIE   You and your turns.
            You and your burns.

BILL   Not any more.
            No burns.

SADIE   No burns.

BILL   Not for ages.
            See?
            See.

SADIE   The urn for the water and the cups for the tea.
            No burns.
            No smashed cups.

BILL   That was Jackie's idea.

SADIE   Aye.

BILL   Are you all right?

SADIE   Apart from I can't breathe.

BILL   Ha.

SADIE   Don't.

BILL   I wasn't.
            You were funny.

SADIE   I wasn't.

BILL   Can you breathe now?

SADIE   …
            Now that you're off me I can.

BILL   …

SADIE   I was funny then.

BILL   You.

SADIE   You.

BILL   It's just a wee hole.

SADIE   I don't want to look.

BILL   There's hardly any glass.

SADIE   I don't want to pick it up.

BILL   I'll get it.

SADIE   Mind your fingers.

BILL   I will.

SADIE   It worked then.
          That new glass.

BILL   Aye.
          Worked fine.
          No cracks.
          Just the one wee hole.

SADIE   Was it a stone?

BILL   Do you want to see it?

SADIE   I don't know.

BILL   It's a stone off the street.

SADIE   Is that what it is?

BILL   That's all it is.
          What did you think?

SADIE   I was thinking it might be worse.

BILL   Like what?

SADIE   I don't know.

BILL   Like a spear?

SADIE   Aye.
          A spear.
          Or an arrow.

BILL   It's a stone.

SADIE   Well that's something.

BILL   And the window's still there.
          Most of it.

SADIE   What if it was a brick?

BILL   Did you see a brick?

SADIE   No.
          But there are bricks.

BILL   In the street?
          Have you seen a brick in the street?

SADIE   No.

BILL   Well why are you speaking about bricks?

SADIE   I know about bricks.

BILL   But there are none in the street.

SADIE   Not now.

BILL   This is a stone off the street.

SADIE   How do you know?

BILL   Look at it.

SADIE   I don't know.

BILL   Look at it.

SADIE   I'm scared.

BILL   It won't bite you.

SADIE   How do you know?

BILL   It's a stone off the street.

SADIE   Are you sure?

BILL   Even if it wasn't a stone off the street, it couldn't
                 bite you.

SADIE   Is that true?

BILL   Aw Sadie.

SADIE   What?

BILL   Stones don't bite.

SADIE   Do they not?

BILL   No.

SADIE   I don't know how you can be so sure.

BILL   I kick them all the time and they never kick back.

SADIE   …

BILL   Have a quick look.

SADIE   Don't make me.

BILL   I'm not making you.

SADIE   Feels like you are.

BILL   I'll not then.
                 You don't have to look.

SADIE   You won't be mad?

BILL   No.

SADIE   Good well.

BILL   I'll put it in the bin.

SADIE   No no.

BILL   How no?

SADIE   It can't stay here.

BILL   In the bin's all right.

SADIE   No no.

BILL   There's a lid on the bin.

SADIE	As long as it's in the house you don't know what might happen.
BILL	I'll take it out with me then.
SADIE	You're not going out.
BILL	Not right now. In a bit.
SADIE	Tomorrow maybe.
BILL	I have to get the bread.
SADIE	I don't think Jackie can come today.
BILL	Don't be daft.
SADIE	I'm not daft. It's a bad day now.
BILL	Just that one thing.
SADIE	But it's a smash. The window.
BILL	She'll never see it.
SADIE	What if the wind blows through it? She'll hear it.
BILL	I'll put a bit of card over it. Tape it up.
SADIE	She'll see that. Even I would see that.
BILL	Only if you were looking.
SADIE	I look at the window.
BILL	I know that.
SADIE	Yes. And I see blue sky.
BILL	It's grey.
SADIE	Or grey.

	Like that today. But not card. I don't see card. Card would look like it didn't belong.
BILL	I know what would fix that.
SADIE	Yes. But he won't come today. He never comes on the same day as the smash.
BILL	We don't need him today. It's just a wee hole.
SADIE	You don't want Jackie to see that smash. She's a worry worry.
BILL	She won't see it.
SADIE	She will if she looks for sky. Blue or grey.
BILL	You wait. You wait and see.
SADIE	Can't keep the curtains closed. We tried that. Looks like somebody died, Jackie said. Don't you be worrying me like that, she said. And anyway it doesn't smell right with the curtains closed all the time. Should we phone Jackie? I don't like the phone. You phone her. She's your niece. She'll think something's up if I phone her. Is everything all right, she'll say That worried way. Is everything all right? So you phone her. What's that? What have you got?
BILL	You watch this.

SADIE   What are you doing?
          What's that?

BILL   Piece of jigsaw puzzle.

SADIE   Did you find it then?

BILL   It's not the missing piece.
          It's a bit of sky.
          See?

SADIE   That's blue.
          The sky's grey.

BILL   I know that.
          I can see that.
          But look now.

SADIE   Blue sky'll work on a sunny day.

BILL   Look at the other side.
          Look.
          Look.

SADIE   It's grey.

BILL   Grey side for rainy day.
          Blue side for sunny day.

SADIE   Sky isn't always that blue.

BILL   We've got hundreds of puzzles.
          We've got hundreds of skies.

SADIE   Ha.

BILL   Eh?

SADIE   You.

BILL   What?

SADIE   You're great.

BILL   Yes I am.

SADIE   What a man.

BILL   See.

SADIE	Some man.
BILL	Aye.
SADIE	What about when it's dark?
BILL	We can shut the curtains when it's dark.
SADIE	Will that be soon?
BILL	I don't think so.
SADIE	What time is it?
BILL	Nearly half two.
SADIE	We've still got time well.
BILL	Yes we do.
SADIE	She wouldn't mind if you called her now.
BILL	No. I'm not calling her.
SADIE	…
BILL	Sadie?
SADIE	…
BILL	Sadie??
SADIE	…
BILL	Don't.
SADIE	…
BILL	What's up?
SADIE	…
BILL	Eh? Eh?
SADIE	I don't like how you said that.
BILL	Said what?
SADIE	I'm not calling her NO.
BILL	I didn't mean it like that.

SADIE   Do you not like me any more?

BILL   Don't be daft.

SADIE   I'm not daft.

BILL   Course I like you.

SADIE   How you said that.
Like my mum.

BILL   No.
Och no.

SADIE   Yes.
Yes.
Just like her.

BILL   No.

SADIE   Yes.
All that.
In your room.
No dinners.
No play.
No toilet.
No getting out.
No bath.
No dinners.
Bad girl.
Smelly girl.
Smelly Sadie.
Just like that.
Yes.

BILL   I didn't mean it like that.

SADIE   I didn't like you then.

BILL   Don't say that.

SADIE   Didn't want to speak to you.

BILL   Do you like me now?

SADIE   I don't know.

BILL   What?

SADIE   Nearly.

BILL   Nearly?

SADIE   I'm nearly done
            Not liking you.

BILL   Well how much longer?

SADIE   …
            …
            Och
            I'm okay now.

BILL   You like me now?

SADIE   You're all right.

BILL   Huh.

SADIE   You don't like it when I don't like you.

BILL   You don't like it when I don't like you.

SADIE   See.

BILL   See what?

SADIE   We're even then.

BILL   Huh.

SADIE   Do you not like that?

BILL   I should be better than you.

SADIE   How?

BILL   I'm the man.

SADIE   Yes you are.

BILL   I should be better.

SADIE   Okay well.

BILL   Okay?

SADIE   It's all one to me.

BILL	Do you want me to phone Jackie?
SADIE	I don't mind.
BILL	Sure?
SADIE	Maybe we won't have toast but, eh?
BILL	I don't mind. Where are you going?
SADIE	I'm not making tea.
BILL	I never asked.
SADIE	It's coming. I'm going to get the jigsaws. We've got some looking to do.
BILL	I'll get them.
SADIE	You can't carry them all.
BILL	We don't need them all. Just the ones with sky.
SADIE	Or grey. There's more than one grey you know.
BILL	I know that.
SADIE	Might even be more greys than blues.
BILL	I know that.
SADIE	Will we need straight edges?
BILL	I don't know.
SADIE	Well you saw the smash hole. Did it have a straight edge?
BILL	No.
SADIE	So no straight edges then.
BILL	… Think you're a clever clogs?
SADIE	Yes.

BILL   Okay.

SADIE   And funny.

BILL   Basil.

SADIE   No.

BILL   Okay.
            I'll get the jigsaws.

SADIE   I'll help you.

BILL   You clear the table.

SADIE   I'll clear the table then.
            Do you want me to leave the picture of your mum
                with the dog?
            Bouncer.
            He's dead.
            I'll put it on the mantel.
            I like it there.
            Just that it's narrow so you can't move it about.
            If you're sitting by the telly you can't see her.
            Jackie says she's dead but you never went to the
                funeral.
            I don't want you to die.
            Hey.
            Hey.
            HEY YOU.
            BILL.
            BILL.

BILL   What's the racket?
            What's all the bloody noise?

SADIE   I don't want you to die.
            Don't swear.

BILL   I'm not dying.
            You make me swear.
            I'm looking at puzzles.

SADIE   Where will I go if you die?

BILL   I'm not dying.

SADIE   But where?

BILL   You might die before me.

SADIE   I won't.

BILL   How do you know?

SADIE   I don't know how.
            I just know.

BILL   Well ta very much.

SADIE   Where will I go?

BILL   You'll stay here.

SADIE   Will they let me?

BILL   It's your house as well as mine.

SADIE   You pay the electric and the bee tee.
            You do all the stuff.
            The rent.
            The pee oh.
            The telly.

BILL   Ellen'll help you.

SADIE   Ellen isn't here all the time.
            Ellen doesn't look up when it rains.

BILL   They can't put you out.

SADIE   Jackie.
            Do you think Jackie will help me?

BILL   Jackie won't be here every day.

SADIE   No she won't.

BILL   She'll only be here now and then.

SADIE   Will she still come when you're dead?

BILL   …

SADIE   …

BILL	Aw Sadie
SADIE	Will she come when you're dead?
BILL	… I'll ask her.
SADIE	What if she says no?
BILL	If I ask her she won't say no.
SADIE	Okay. Ask her then.
BILL	Will you be sad when I die?
SADIE	Don't ask.
BILL	How no?
SADIE	Because I don't know.
BILL	What?
SADIE	It never happened before.
BILL	Are you being funny?
SADIE	No.
BILL	Are you being a clever clogs?
SADIE	No.
BILL	Are you going to sort these puzzles then?
SADIE	Aye. Do you want all the blues even seas and lochs and rivers and puddles and what's that, ponds? Do you want them all?
BILL	I don't know.
SADIE	You should know.
BILL	How?
SADIE	You're the man is how.
BILL	Right then. Just sky then.

SADIE   Sky it is, Captain.

BILL   Captain.

SADIE   That's funny.

BILL   I like Captain.

SADIE   Aye.

         What about the greys?

BILL   What about the greys, Captain?

SADIE   What about the greys?
         Captain.

BILL   My mother was a grey.

SADIE   I never met her.
         Just the picture.
         And Bouncer.
         Bouncer looks like a lot of dogs.

BZZZZZZZZZZZZZZ
ZZZZZZZZZZZZZZZ

Oo.

BILL   That'll be Jackie.

SADIE   Get the buzzer.

BILL   Put the puzzles away first.

BZZZ BZZ BZZ

SADIE   The buzzer.

BILL   Mind the puzzles.

SADIE   What about the window?

BILL   Never mind the window.

SADIE   Pull the curtain.
         That's what.

BILL   It's not dark.
              She'll think we're not in.

BZZZZZZ

              She'll think we're not in.

SADIE   Will you get the buzzer?

BILL   I'll get it.

SADIE   Right.
              Right then.

BILL   Put away the puzzles then.

SADIE   In the back room?

Bzz zz

BILL   JUST PUT THEM BY

SADIE   I'm going.
              I'm going.

BILL   I'll get the door.

SADIE   Let me get by first.

BILL   Go go.

              SADIE *and* BILL *get stuck in the door.*

              SADIE *pushes and panics.*

              The jigsaws fall.

SADIE   …
              …
              Oh.
              Oh.
              …
              Oh

BILL   Ach.
              Dumbo.
              Dumbo.

SADIE	They fell.
BILL	She'll leave. Thickie. Dumbo.
SADIE	Aah. Don't. Aw. Don't YOU.
BILL	…
SADIE	…
BILL	…
SADIE	…

No buzzer.

BILL	She's away.
SADIE	It wasn't my fault.
BILL	You're too fat.
SADIE	I know. Will I pick them up?
BILL	And clumsy.
SADIE	Sorry. Sorry.
BILL	You need to go on a diet.
SADIE	…
BILL	Thickie.
SADIE	…
BILL	I'll have to go after her.
SADIE	Will you?
BILL	Don't ask.
SADIE	Right well.

BILL   I'll need to get my coat.

SADIE   Chinny chin chin again.
            Finnegan.
            Finnegan that's who.

BILL   I'll have to go.

SADIE   What if it wasn't her?

BILL   Who else?

SADIE   I don't know.
            People come.
            The postman.

BILL   We'd hear if it was the postman.
            Scliffing up the stairs.

SADIE   Somebody else then.

BILL   What if it was her?

SADIE   She'd be worried.

BILL   Aye.

SADIE   She'd be in the street.

BILL   Come away from the window.

SADIE   Right.

BILL   Right.

SADIE   You look then.

BILL   Right then.
            I will.

SADIE   Just a bit.
            Just a peek.

BILL   I can't see round the corner.

SADIE   Maybe she'll telephone.

BILL   She won't telephone.

SADIE   How no?

BILL	Because she knows we don't answer it.
SADIE	She might leave a message.
BILL	She knows you're scared of the phone. She won't phone.
SADIE	…
BILL	I'll have to go after her.
SADIE	…
BILL	Coat then.
SADIE	I'll get it.
BILL	Furry hood.
SADIE	I know that.
BILL	Basil.
SADIE	Don't.
BILL	Maybe it wasn't her.
SADIE	Maybe.
BILL	But I'll need to go and look.
SADIE	Okay.
BILL	I may as well get bread. Eh?
SADIE	How long will you be?
BILL	Quick if I find her and slow if I don't.
SADIE	How long?
BILL	Maybe half an hour.
SADIE	How will I know when it's half an hour?
BILL	I don't know.
SADIE	You're the man you said. Captain.

BILL   As long as the bus into the town.
            And back.

SADIE   Okay.

BILL   Don't open the door.

SADIE   Don't worry.
            What if Jackie comes while you're away?

BILL   I'll see her.
            If it's Jackie she'll be with me.
            And I've got my keys.

SADIE   Keys.

BILL   Wallet.

SADIE   No door.

BILL   No phone.

SADIE   No door no phone.

BILL   I better go.

SADIE   Keys.
            Wallet.
            No door no phone.
            Bus into the town.
            And back.

BILL   Right.

SADIE   Will it stop at all the stops?

BILL   I don't know.

SADIE   …?

BILL   Do I?

SADIE   Well it's one time if it doesn't stop but another
            time if it does.

BILL   It'll stop at all the stops.

SADIE   Okay.

BILL   Lock the door at my back.

SADIE   I know how to lock the door.
              I'm not daft.

BILL   Now then.

SADIE   Hurry up and get out then.

              *A quiet closing of the door followed by keys turned
              slowly.* SADIE *draws the bolts noiselessly.*

              I'm getting on the bus now, Bill.
              No queue.
              Can you believe it?
              Room at the front.
              Sit sit quick.
              There we are.
              Look at the shoes.
              No shoes today.
              The bus is empty, Bill.
              I've got my pick of seats today.
              …
              Ding.
              Stopping.
              Nobody at the stop.
              Ding.
              First stop.
              Costcutters.
              Buggy and fags.
              Not today.
              No traffic, Bill.
              No shoes no bags.
              Is it the lady driver, I don't know.
              I'll not get up to see while it's moving, Bill, eh?
              I'll wait till I'm getting off, that's what you say.
              …
              Ding.
              Stopping.
              William Hill.
              Bill Hill, you say.
              Bill Hill it would be if it was me.

Cans and fags.
Spit.
Not today.
I'm looking up today, Bill.
You should see me.
Back and front.
Wide as you like.
No spit.
Costcutters.
William Hill.
…
Ding.
Stopping.
That'll be the Forge / next stop

BEEDLYDEEP.
BEEDLYDEEP.

Ee.

BEEDLYDEEP.
BEEDLYDEEP.

No phone.

BEEDLYDEEP.
BEEDLYDEEP.

No phone no door.

BEEDLYDEEP.
BEEDLYDEEP.

Jackie won't call.
It won't be Jackie.
…
Stay on the bus.
It stops at every stop.

All the way to the town.
And back.

BEEEEEEP.

BILL	Sadie. Sadie.
SADIE	I'm on the bus, Bill. Like you said.
BILL	Sadie, I'm in a phone box.
SADIE	Are you?
BILL	Sadie, will you pick up the phone?
SADIE	No phone no door.
BILL	Sadie, can you hear me?
SADIE	I can hear / you fine.
BILL	Sadie, if you can hear me, will you pick up the phone.
SADIE	No I will not.
BILL	I forgot my key, Sadie. I looked in my pocket and the keys weren't in it.
SADIE	I said keys. Wallet.
BILL	Sadie, pick up the phone.
SADIE	No door no phone.
BILL	Sadie, it's me here.
SADIE	Bill, it's me here.
BILL	Can you see the red button, Sadie?
SADIE	I'm not blind. Do you think / I'm blind?
BILL	You can press the button, Sadie. It's not the same as picking up the phone.

SADIE	Stay on the bus.
BILL	Press the button.
SADIE	Every stop.
BILL	We never said anything about the button.
SADIE	You said to stay on the bus. No / door no phone.
BILL	Sadie, I promise nothing bad will happen if you press the button.

bee

Press it right in, Sadie.
So I can hear you.

BILL	. . . Sadie.
SADIE	I can hear you.
BILL	I can hear you.
SADIE	What are you doing?
BILL	I'm in the phone box.
SADIE	What are you in the phone box for?
BILL	I forgot my key.
SADIE	Do you want me to find it?
BILL	No.
SADIE	Okay.
BILL	You'll have to let me in.
SADIE	The now?
BILL	When I come back.
SADIE	Where are you?

BILL   I'm in the phone box.
            I'm going to come home.

SADIE   Come home then.
            Don't be in the phone box.

BILL   You'll have to let me in.

SADIE   Okay.

BILL   Okay?

SADIE   You forgot your key.

BILL   I know.
            I'll buzz the buzzer.

SADIE   Okay.

BILL   I'll be quick.

SADIE   Right, Captain.

BILL   I'm going to hang up now.

SADIE   Right.

beedeep

Am I to get back on the bus?
Bill?

beep

Press the button.
Press the button.
Am I to get back on the bus, Bill?
You never said.
And I don't remember what stop I was at.
Costcutters.
Yes.
Yes.
Costcutters and then.
Thingy.
Thingy.
Cans.

Spit.
Bill Hill.
I can't hear you.
I'm not on the bus any more, Bill.

…

…

Don't know how long the time is, well.
Ding.
Not on the bus any more.

BEEDLYDEEP
BEEDLYDEEP

Oh. Oh.

BEEDLYDEEP
BEEDLYDEEP

I don't know.

I don't know.

BEEDLYDEEP
BEEDLYDEEP

Button button.

Red button.

BEEDLYDEEP
BEEDLYDEEP

Nobody said anything about the button.
Button.
Bill.
Bill.
How long will you be?
You never said.

BOY   Ya fucking fat-arsed spastic.

SADIE   Wha?
           Wha?
           Oh.
           Oh.

BOY   Fucking in on your own aren't you, Spazo.
           Fucking coming to get you.
           Fucking ugly cow.
           Moo.
           Moo.
           Spastic fucking cow.
           Moooooo.
           Your fucking weirdo boyfriend's no' in.
           I've just seen him.
           That means you're by yourself.
           And I'm coming to get you.
           You get yourself ready.

SADIE   Nononononononononononononononononononononono
           nonononono

BOY   Because I feel like a wank.
           Gonny wank all over your fat fucking minge face,
               Mingebreath...

SADIE   Nonononononononononononononononononononono
           nonononono

BOY   ...and then when I'm done I'm gonny pee on you.
           Maybe take a shite and then wipe myself wi your
               hair.

SADIE   AAAAAAAAAAAAAAAAAAAAAAAAAA
           AAAAAAAAAAAAAAA
           AAAAAAAAAAAAAAAAAAAAAAAAAAAAAA

BOY   Get yourself ready.

           Mooooo.

           *Panic. Phone up. Phone down. Panic. Chair in the
           way. Tumble. Oh shit. Oh shit.*

BZZZZZZZ

SADIE   Ohhhhhhhhhhhhhhhhhhhhhhhhhhhhhhhhhhhhhhhhh

BILL.
BILL.
I GOT OFF THE BUS
SORRY SORRY
BILL.

BZZZZ BZZZZZ
BZZZZZ BZ BZ

BZ

SADIE runs to open the door. But it isn't BILL. *A* BOY *drags her by the hair back into her living room.* SADIE *curls up in a ball to protect herself. He puts his foot lightly on her head.*

BOY   Tell me you love me, Skank.

SADIE   Mummydaddymummydaddymummydaddy
mummydaddy

The BOY *unzips his trousers and waves his penis above her face.*

BOY   Tell me you love me.

SADIE   Mummydaddymummydaddymummydaddy
mummydaddy

BOY   You are
One
Ugly
Minge.

He pees on her.

SADIE   Mummydaddymummydaddymummydaddy
mummydaddy

BOY   Look at me when I'm talking to you.

             Look at me.

             He pees on her face. He lifts his foot and stamps on her head.

PLAY TWO

In a bar.

DAVE   There was a call for you.

JACKIE   For me?
          I don't think so.

DAVE   It was your son.

JACKIE   No.
          Not my son.
          Wouldn't have been my son.

DAVE   You're the only Jackie who works here.

JACKIE   He doesn't have this number.

DAVE   He does now.

JACKIE   When did he call?
          He has my mobile numb / Did he ask for me by
              name?
          What did he say?
          Why didn't you tell me?

DAVE   Woah.
          He didn't want to talk to you.

JACKIE   …

DAVE   Why don't you leave that?
          The cleaner gets paid to do it.

JACKIE   What did he say, exactly?
          My son.

DAVE   He said, I'd like to leave a message for Jackie
              please.

JACKIE   …
           Jackie?
           Like that?
           Just Jackie?

DAVE   That's what he said.
           He was very polite.

JACKIE   He's a good…
           I mean…

DAVE   I offered to get you.

JACKIE   Yes?

DAVE   I said, do you want to speak to her?
           She's right here.

JACKIE   Where was I?

DAVE   Right here.

JACKIE   But where?

DAVE   I looked round for you and you were here.
           Right here.
           Hereabouts.
           Putting the glasses away.

JACKIE   And I didn't hear you?

DAVE   I asked him if he wanted a word.
           He said no.
           He said, I don't want to disturb her.
           Tell her when she's finished her shift.

JACKIE   Uhuh?

DAVE   I just want to leave her a message.

JACKIE   You're lying.

DAVE   Why?

JACKIE   I know you are.

DAVE   I might be making the most of it but I'm not lying.
           Just let me get a pencil, I said to him.

JACKIE   And all this time, I never heard a thing?
          Never noticed you on the phone?
          …
          Making the most of it?

DAVE   It was noisy.
          You were emptying the glass washer.
          …
          I like you.

JACKIE   I would have noticed if you were on the phone to
              my son.

DAVE   How?

JACKIE   I don't know.
          I just know.

DAVE   It was over in a flash.

JACKIE   You went to get a pencil, you said.

DAVE   No.
          I didn't.
          He said, you won't need a pencil.
          You'll remember it.

JACKIE   …?

DAVE   He said, can you tell my mum that today is a good
              day.

JACKIE   …

DAVE   Today is a good day.
          What d'you make of that?

JACKIE   …

DAVE   Hey.
          Hey.
          Shit.
          What's wrong?
          Jeezus.
          What is it?

JACKIE   Don't you
          Don't you say that to me if it isn't
          If it isn't the gospel fucking truth.

DAVE   Jeesus.
          Jackie.

JACKIE   Don't you dare
          You fucking
          Don't you
          Dare.

DAVE   I'm not.
          I didn't.
          I wouldn't.

JACKIE   …

DAVE   Would you put the brush down?

JACKIE   I don't know.

DAVE   Put it down.

JACKIE   Say it again.

DAVE   Today's a good day.

JACKIE   The whole thing.
          The way he said it.

DAVE   Can you tell my mum that today is a good day.

JACKIE   …
          …
          …

DAVE   Jesus, Jackie, you'd think somebody had died.

JACKIE   …

DAVE   Can I get you something?

JACKIE   Kitchen roll.

DAVE   Right.
          Right.

JACKIE   He said it.

DAVE   Today is a good day.

JACKIE   He's having a good day.

DAVE   I don't think he meant to make you cry.

JACKIE   It's not crying.

DAVE   No?

JACKIE   It's more a kind of
         Running over.

DAVE   Okay.
         Running over.

JACKIE   Tell my mum that today is a good day.

DAVE   Is it not usually a good day?

JACKIE   For other people.
         Maybe.
         I don't know.

DAVE   …?
         …
         What are you going to do with it?

JACKIE   I don't know.
         I don't know.
         I didn't plan on it.

DAVE   Shame to waste it.
         Shame to know you've got a good day and let it
            go to waste.

JACKIE   I shouldn't waste a good day.

DAVE   You should celebrate.

JACKIE   Have you any idea what.
         …
         Yes.
         I should celebrate.

DAVE   What can I tempt you with?

JACKIE   Maybe I won't.

DAVE   There you go.
            Day over in less than a minute.

JACKIE   Sorry.
            It's a nice gesture.
            I'm
            I promised my uncle I'd visit him today.

DAVE   Your uncle?

JACKIE   He goes to a lot of trouble.

DAVE   Uncles can be visited any time.
            That's an ordinary day, the visiting uncle day.

JACKIE   I don't visit them as much as I should.

DAVE   At least you go.
            I've got family who don't even know I'm alive.

JACKIE   They're…
            I should go.

DAVE   And yet you stay.

JACKIE   Ha.

DAVE   You don't really want to go.

JACKIE   I'm.
            It's a bit of a.
            They make tea and cold.
            It's not just that.
            It's that
            I have the horrible feeling that if I leave
            When I leave here
            The good day will be gone.

DAVE   That's right that's right.
            The good day was delivered by messenger to this
                    establishment.
            The good day takes place here.
            Red or white?

JACKIE	That's magical thinking, isn't it? Good luck bad luck signs and omens. The good day is a good day anywhere. Right? I'm rubbish.
DAVE	You can't talk about my staff like that.
JACKIE	I'm having a good day and I don't know what to do with it.
DAVE	Give it room. Let it sink in.
JACKIE	What would you do on a good day?
DAVE	…
JACKIE	?
DAVE	First thought or second thought?
JACKIE	Second, I think.
DAVE	I'd drive to the coast. I'd get in my car. The rain would stop. The car would start, first time and I'd drive until I got to the coast.
JACKIE	Which coast?
DAVE	There's only one coast. The west coast.
JACKIE	It's winter.
DAVE	And I'd do that thing I've been promising myself I'd do since I was, I don't know, seventeen. I'd take off my gear and run into the water.
JACKIE	Seventeen. What about swimming stuff?
DAVE	I'd find a cove.
JACKIE	A cove.

DAVE   Wouldn't matter.
            I'm not worrying about all the things that usually
                stop me – swimming stuff, people watching,
                the cold sea, even rain if it had to.
            Because it's a good day, right?

JACKIE   So far.

DAVE   I'd get in that water and I'd feel alive.
            Really alive.
            Freezing your balls off alive because that's what
                you want on a good day isn't it?
            You want to feel the most alive.
            Feel something amazing.
            So amazing that when it stops being the good day
                you can still remember the good day feeling.
            Even if you were frozen.
            Right?

JACKIE   It doesn't sound so impossible.

DAVE   It doesn't.
            Don't know why I haven't done it before.
            What do you think?

JACKIE   What?

DAVE   Shut the bar and go.

JACKIE   Ha.

DAVE   Yeah?
            Yeah?

JACKIE   It's
            Winter.
            Freezing.
            Raining, like you said.

DAVE   Yeah, yeah, yeah.
            Well?

JACKIE   Could we do that?

DAVE   I'm the boss.

JACKIE   I promised my uncle.
            They're expecting me.
            It wouldn't be fair.

DAVE   Call him.

JACKIE   They don't like.
            It's too.
            They're not so great with sudden change.
            Or telephones.

DAVE   One day.
            One good day.
            Who knows when the next one will be?

JACKIE   …
            Shit.

DAVE   I said the wrong thing.

JACKIE   Tomorrow will be another bad day.

DAVE   Might be loads of good days.
            Loads eh?
            You never / know.

JACKIE   Do you know how long I've been waiting for this
                good day?

DAVE   I don't know.
            Good days / can be hard to come by.

JACKIE   Four-and-a-half years.
            Four-and-a-half years was the last good day.

DAVE   Long wait.
            This is an up-turn then.
            A definite up-turn.

JACKIE   I didn't know it was my last good day.
            It wasn't even all that good.
            I had a cold, flu, one of those, viruses.
            We both had it.

DAVE   It must mean something then.
            This day.

This very special good day.

JACKIE   Yes.
This day is good.
Yes.
You're right.

DAVE   Yes, sir.
Let's strike it while it's hot then.
Shut up shop and drive to the coast.

JACKIE   You're on.

DAVE   Wee glass to see us on our way.

JACKIE   On you go then.

DAVE   You usually have a Sauvignon Blanc.
Marlborough?

JACKIE   I thought we were celebrating.
I'll have the Sancerre.

DAVE   I'll have to open a fresh bottle.

JACKIE   Na never mind.
I wouldn't want you to –

DAVE   I.
That was.
Shit.
Reflex.
Didn't even think.
Shit.
Good day good vino.
Right?

JACKIE   We don't have to.
It doesn't matter.

DAVE   I knew it.
Don't say that.
I knew.
Soon as the words were out my mouth.
Have to open a fresh bottle.

Wanker.
Wanker.
It's.
You know.
That's me.
I'm not saying it's not
Part of me.
It's training.
It's not that I'm.
I have a generous spirit.
Look.
Please.
Let me open the Sancerre.
Fuck.
I'll.
It'll be a punishment if you don't.
I'll feel punished.
Here you are.
There we are.
Look.
It's opened.

JACKIE   I'll buy the rest of the Sancerre.
Don't worry.
I wouldn't expect you to
I'll buy it and take it home.

DAVE   It'll keep.
Somebody will come in tomorrow and decide that
it's his special day and he'll buy his girlfriend
a large glass of Sancerre and she'll love it so
he'll buy her more.
We'll probably have to open another bottle.
For sure.
I can tell.
It's that kind of day.
That kind of week.
I had it first hand, from your son.

JACKIE   A good day.

DAVE   What's his name?

JACKIE   Oh I don't
             You don't want to know all that stuff.

DAVE   Okay.

JACKIE   When he said Jackie
             How did he sound?
             Did he sound embarrassed to be saying that?

DAVE   I don't know.
             Maybe.
             It was loud in the bar.

JACKIE   You ever hear your children call you Dave?

DAVE   No.
             They don't call me that.

JACKIE   …
             Your children don't call you.

DAVE   Ha.
             What a thing to
             Say.

JACKIE   In the three months I've been here they've never
                  called.

DAVE   My children are.

JACKIE   You don't see your children.

DAVE   Maybe I don't have any.

JACKIE   Is that a joke?
             Is that your idea of a joke?

DAVE   I'm sliding here, Jackie.
             You know.
             It's.
             I'm very glad it's a good day.
             I've had them before to tell you the truth.
             But
             You won't tell me the name of your son and you
             Well

You know
You comment
About my children
It's
Slippy ground
I'm not used to being caught off – [guard].
Not in here.
Do you like the Sancerre?

JACKIE His name is Nicholas.
Nick.
Due on Christmas Day.
Irresistible really.
Nicholas.
Bit obvious.
His father chose it.
That or Noel.
Couldn't help thinking about telly Noels.
Crossroads.
Swap Shop.
Well.
I've met a few Nicks.
Always liked them.
Never met a bad Nick.

DAVE Nice Christmas present.

JACKIE Christmas present my arse.
Didn't turn up until the tenth of January.
I was starting to panic.
Terrified he was going to be an Aquarius.

DAVE I don't see my children.

JACKIE That's a shame.

DAVE They're better off.

JACKIE Do they know that?

DAVE …
Do you want to get pissed?
Jackie?

JACKIE	Most days. I try to resist.
DAVE	Do you want to get pissed today?
JACKIE	I don't know.
DAVE	What would help you make up your mind?
JACKIE	I'm not sure it's the right thing. I've been pissed a lot. It doesn't help.
DAVE	Sure. When you're low, pissed takes you lower. But this is not a low day.
JACKIE	I was. I'm trying to. I've been getting on top of it.
DAVE	As long as that's the only thing you've been getting on top of.
JACKIE	Now you're worrying me.
DAVE	Joke. Joke. Wee pun. Pun and a half.
JACKIE	I'm not so sure about you.
DAVE	Me? Drinking with a friend when you're drinking with me.
JACKIE	Even if I got drunk, Dave. I wouldn't suck your dick.
DAVE	Whu… Hu… Did I ask you? Woah. Did I even Jesus Christ on a bike, man

You're way WAY way off.
Suck my
I can't even
How do you even find the
Jesus
The words?

JACKIE   I'm not doing it.

DAVE   I didn't ask.

JACKIE   It was coming.

DAVE   Not for a long time.
Not for a very long
Jeessus.
Maybe even years, for Christ's…
Man.

JACKIE   It's just

DAVE   …?

JACKIE   I've given this some thought, Dave, and the truth
is, I don't think I really like the penis.

DAVE   Jesus.
Fuck's sake, Jackie.
Let me finish one mouthful before you say
anything else.

JACKIE   I think I've always been a bit
Well
A bit disturbed by the
The
By the way they.
You know
The vagina…

DAVE   Fuuuck

JACKIE   …is tucked away.
I'm not saying it isn't grotesque in its own way
But you know
It's not making a song and dance about it.

Whereas the penis

DAVE   I wish you'd stop saying that.
        I'm beginning to wish I didn't have one.

JACKIE The penis.
        It well.
        Well it's.
        It sticks out.

DAVE   …

JACKIE Spear-like.
        Full of
        Charge.
        CHARGE.

DAVE   …

JACKIE And semen.

DAVE   It's how we're built.
        It's engineering.
        You can't

JACKIE Sometimes / I can't believe I've done all the
              things with a penis that I've actually done.
        Like I'm a survivor of a terrible plane crash where
              we had to eat everybody else so we could
              live.
        It's that
        Alien / No.
        Absurd.

DAVE   Well, as long as you had fun.

JACKIE I don't know.
        I don't really remember.
        I think I was probably drunk.

DAVE   You an alcoholic, Jack?

JACKIE I don't think so.

DAVE   Don't take this the wrong way
        But do you think you could be gay?

JACKIE   I don't think so.
           I'm not saying I haven't had the odd same-sex
               dream
           But only when I was
           Only when it had been a while.
           No.
           I don't like the penis to look at but I do like
               penetration.
           Have you ever licked a vagina?

DAVE   Yes I have
           Thank you for asking.

JACKIE   Did it not taste funny?

DAVE   Funny Ha Ha?

JACKIE   You know.

DAVE   Yes I have licked a
           A vgina.
           I don't have a particularly good sense of taste so
               while I could identify notes of seashells, yeast
               and possibly traces of pish I don't think hand on
               my heart I can do full justice to your question.

JACKIE   Yeah yeah.
           But did you like it?

DAVE   I don't.

JACKIE   Well did you?

DAVE   Yes.
           Yes I did.
           Like it very much indeed.
           But then I wasn't really in thinking mode.
           You know?
           And it was more than once.

JACKIE   A lot?

DAVE   Do you want me to lick you?
           Is that why you're asking?
           Is that what you want me to do?

JACKIE   Not today.

DAVE   Is this?
Are you?
What's the?
Are we?
Done?

JACKIE   Yes yes.
I'm not sure.
I don't know.
I just wanted to be clear about the penis / thing

DAVE   Clear as a bell.
Couldn't be clearer.

JACKIE   Just that
There are times you know
When things are not clear
You can find yourself in all sorts of.
Before you know it
You've given a wrong signal
And wham.
How do you get out of that?

DAVE   You've been very clear.

JACKIE   You'll probably just want me to go home now, eh?

DAVE   If that's what you / want.

JACKIE   Probably spoiled your whole day with all this /
          babble.

DAVE   No no.
Well.
I'm not.
It's been.
Well.
Now that you mention it
It's been very
Stimulating
Not in that way.
I mean

So far.
In fact
From the moment your son called the day took on
    a new
Sheen.

JACKIE   That's right.
That's exactly him.
He can do that.
He has a light.
He's beautiful, you know.
You don't know him but he's
Everybody says this about him
He's –

DAVE   …

JACKIE   Sorry.
Sorry.

DAVE   …

JACKIE   …

DAVE   I'm sure he's a lovely / boy.

JACKIE   He is.
He is.
And polite.
People talk about him as if he's
One of a kind.
…
…
But they don't hear the bad days.
The days when he almost doesn't live.
They don't hear that.
The endless days when he can't move because of
    the pain.
Can't get to classes.
Can't buy food.
The days I keep checking up on him.
Just in case.
Just in case.

How high is his window?
I ask myself.
Stupid things like that.
Is he driving too fast?
How can he bear it when he doesn't know if he's
     ever going to get better?
Nobody hears that.
Except me.
He keeps that for me.
He calls me because he can talk to me.
Let off steam.
He can talk to me.
But he doesn't know.
The thing he doesn't
Didn't know is
Was
I couldn't hear it any more.
I said to him.
I didn't really mean it.
It was a bad day.
A long run of very bad days.
I would have been better another day.
I snapped at him.
I didn't mean it.
But my heart you know
My heart just plummets
So low
So low like
Like.
No matter how low you've felt
No matter what's actually happened to you
When something happens to them
There's a whole fucking
TRAPDOOR
A whole other world
Of low
That you never knew anything about.
Sorry.
Sorry but

Sadness
Real sadness is not being able to help your child
        when they're in pain.
Doesn't matter what they've got.
You don't care about that.
You just want them to stop hurting.
And I know that.
I should know that.
But I said to him, son
SON
Please.
Just once
Just one time
Will you call me and tell me when you're having a
        good day.
JUST ONCE.

DAVE   Today.

JACKIE   And it was like I'd mortally wounded him.
            Like
            The only support
            The only person he could rely on had gone.
            Vanished.
            Worse than that
            Worse
            Had slapped him before she went.
            And then
            Nothing.
            You know what's worse than bad news?
            No news.
            No news unless I phone and ask
            How are you, son?
            How's it been?
            Are you coping, son?
            Will you call me, sweetheart?
            Doesn't matter how you feel
            Just call.
            For years, you know
            Years – ever since he was born

I've told him
How great he is
How much I love him
How no matter whatever happens I'll still be here.
Must be every day for years.
And one time
ONE TIME
I say something else and that's all he remembers.
I've been.
I can't say.
Lost my job.
Gave my job up.
I'm a nurse
I'm a bloody good nurse.
I can look after people.
Not just look after them.
You come in to A and E on a Friday night
You're bleeding
You're drunk
You want to hurt somebody.
See me?
I can calm you down.
I can figure out what's wrong
Where you're hurt
I can fix you.
Almost always.
I'm the woman you want to be there when you're
    hurt.
But I stopped caring.
I couldn't look after other people any more.
Nothing left.
In they'd troop
Bleeding
Broken
Horrible terrible-looking states
And I found myself thinking
Well why don't you just die, ya bastards?
You're not taking care of your life.
You're pissing it up the wall and expecting
    somebody

Me

Expecting me to patch you up.

I thought it would pass but then I found myself not
worrying if I hurt them while I was fixing
them.

Sure sign it's time to go.

Somewhere in me, I care.

Can't find it.

So I had to have a job that doesn't matter

No offence.

I have to have a job with fixed hours.

No homework.

Nothing worse than a broken glass or bit of
spillage to worry me.

…

I'm a bit rubbish these days.

DAVE   …

?

…

You're very good behind the bar.

JACKIE   Yeah?

DAVE   I'd hate to lose you.

JACKIE   Lose me?

DAVE   But I would understand.

You know

Day'll come I'm sure

The day'll come when you'll want to go back to
your real life

Your proper job.

Nobody sticks around here for long.

You can do a good job.

An important.

All I'm saying is

Come that day.

When you leave.

I'll be

I'll understand.

JACKIE   I wasn't thinking of going quite yet.

DAVE   No?

JACKIE   No.
           Not yet.
           I've got
           Bills to pay.
           And stuff.
           Endless stuff.
           Mortgage.
           Gas electricity.

DAVE   Utilities.

JACKIE   Yes.
           Utilities.

DAVE   Good.
           Good.

JACKIE   Council tax.

DAVE   I don't think you're rubbish.

JACKIE   Trust me.
           I'm.
           I don't even remember specifics any more.
           Just get up in the morning.
           Do the day.
           Go to sleep.
           Get up the next morning.
           …
           That's a very nice Sancerre.

DAVE   Yeah.
           Yeah.
           Here.

JACKIE   I need to go.

DAVE   Come on.
           Come on.
           You're just relaxing into it.

JACKIE   I know.
          That's not a good thing.

DAVE   It is.
          Today it is.

JACKIE   I have to go in a minute.

DAVE   You don't.

JACKIE   I do.
          It'll be on my mind.
          I won't be.
          I have to go.

DAVE   What'll you do there?

JACKIE   I'll eat cold toast and cheese.
          They make the same things every time.
          They make it before I come so they can sit and
               talk to me.
          God knows how long it takes them.
          I'm sure they get up early.
          I don't even like toast and cheese.
          I think I did when I was little.
          I haven't the heart to tell them.
          And they ask me if I want tomato sauce and I say
               yes even though I don't want it and we laugh.
          And they tell me the same things.
          How they like their plastic cups.
          How they got Garibaldi biscuits in just for me.
          How they keep the urn on all day so they can have
               a cup of tea whenever they want.
          How great the freezer is.
          Do I want ice cream.
          More tea.
          They'll keep looking out of the window to see if
               it's getting dark.
          I'll wonder when I can go.
          They'll ask me when I'm going.
          We'll look at the picture of my grandmother and
               the dog.

> Sadie will say
> I never met her.
> Just the dog.
> Bouncer.
> And Bill will laugh at her
> And nudge me to laugh at her too.
> And then I'll have another cup of tea
> But I won't drink it all
> Because they'll be getting worried now about how
>   I'll get home in the dark.
> So I'll go.
> And I'll feel as if I didn't give them enough time.
> And they'll wave at me from the window.
> Sadie always waves till I'm out of sight.
> I have to keep turning round to
> Wave at her.

DAVE   They sound…

JACKIE   Yeah.
          They are.

DAVE   …nice

JACKIE   Yes.
          Yes.
          Really nice.
          You can see why I have to go.

DAVE   Yeah.
          Yeah.
          You should go.
          Sounds like they'll miss you if you don't.

JACKIE   Oh God yes.

DAVE   But it's early yet.

JACKIE   They'll be waiting.

DAVE   Woah.
          You can't gulp a good glass of wine.

JACKIE   I know.

Sorry.
I meant what I said about paying / for

DAVE   Please.
You'll hurt my feelings.

JACKIE   Right.
Coat bag gloves.
Brolly.
Bloody miserable out there.

DAVE   You're forgetting.

JACKIE   No.
I'm not.
I remember.
It's a good day.

DAVE   Yes it is.

JACKIE   I know.
Just the weather that's bad.
I know.

DAVE   Don't come in tonight.
Do something
Fun.

JACKIE   No no.
I'll come in.
I like it.
I like the company.

DAVE   Yeah?

JACKIE   Shutup.

DAVE   Whatever.
I can get cover.
You
Take care.

JACKIE   Will do.
…

DAVE   Maybe they'll find a cure.

JACKIE   Oh.
          Maybe.
          I
          I don't think like that any more.

DAVE   No.

JACKIE   …

DAVE   …

JACKIE   What was…?

DAVE   …
          What was what?

JACKIE   Your first thought.
          You know you said
          First thought or second thought.

DAVE   Oh.
          That.
          …

JACKIE   …?

DAVE   That was the version where we both get naked and
              run into the sea.

JACKIE   …

DAVE   And laugh and
          Fight that thing.
          That freezing wave.
          Beat it.
          And then we run out but we can't heat up.
          Not on our own.
          Can't warm your own back, can you?
          You need some help with that.
          So we rub each other to keep warm.
          To warm up.

JACKIE   …

DAVE   I rub my hands up and down your arms and your
              back and

Because.

JACKIE   It's cold.

DAVE   Freezing.

JACKIE   I'd be numb with the cold.
This weather.

DAVE   I'd be thinking how long it's been
Since I've done that
And how much I miss the touch of
Someone
In that
Privileged way.
The way it is when you have access to someone.
To touch someone.
How some days
Apart from the feel of fingers on a glass
Or when I'm passed the money
Some days I don't touch anyone.
I.

JACKIE   Yeah.

DAVE   And you rub your hands up and down my arms
Even though I'm not that cold any more
Which is just as well because you've no strength
     at all.
I'd freeze to death waiting for you to warm me up.
But I stand there and let you all the same.

JACKIE   I'm not such a weakling.

DAVE   …

JACKIE   …

DAVE   And then of course that's when you lie on top of
     me and sit on my face.

JACKIE   …

DAVE   That was my first thought.

JACKIE   Why didn't you say that?

DAVE   I didn't know you well enough back then.

JACKIE   …

DAVE   Why don't you call them?

JACKIE   …

DAVE   Car's round the back.

JACKIE   It's pouring.

DAVE   It's winter.

JACKIE   I don't.
            I'm not that.
            You know.
            Even if we did
            I wouldn't want to take my clothes
            Off.
            Not yet I / don't think

DAVE   We could just
            Go for a drive up to Balmaha and
            Have a cup of tea.

JACKIE   Oh.
            Right.

DAVE   If that's what you want.
            Nothing we do on this day is wrong.
            Whatever we choose.
            No blame.
            No judgement.
            It's just what we do.

JACKIE   …

DAVE   Come on.
            Don't wait.
            Do it now.

JACKIE   Okay.
            Okay.
            I'm.
            I am.

I'm going to do it.
Yes.
Yes.
I'll have to call.
They hate the phone.
I'll have to call.
They won't answer.

…

I'll call.
I'll call then.
Hang on.

beep beep beep beep

beep beep beep

beep beep beep beep

Hello hello.
Uncle Bill.
Sadie.
Hello.
It's me.
Pick up the phone.
Hello hello hello.
Listen.
I'm
I can't come today.
I'm sorry.
I've
I've been
Asked to
To work and I don't feel I can say no.
Sorry.
Sorry sorry.
It was
It came out of the blue.
I'll come at the weekend.
Saturday.
I'll come early.
I'll be there by eleven.

We'll have the whole day.
That'll be good eh?
Maybe even go into Marks and Spencer's café
Have a bit of Victoria sponge.
You'd like that, Sadie
Wouldn't you?
We'll do that on Saturday.
I'm sorry.
Hope you're not too disappointed.
I know you go to a lot of trouble.
Hope you haven't already made the toast.
But the Garibaldis'll keep.
I'll see you soon.
Lots of love.
Bye.
Bye.
It's Jackie.
If you can hear me.
Jackie.
Bye.
Bye then.

DAVE   Okay?

JACKIE   They didn't pick up.
They're probably in, you know.
I knew they wouldn't answer.
They never pick up.

End.

A Nick Hern Book

Any Given Day first published in Great Britain as a paperback original in 2010
by Nick Hern Books Limited, 14 Larden Road, London W3 7ST
in association with the Traverse Theatre, Edinburgh

Any Given Day copyright © 2010 Linda McLean

Cover image by Laurence Winram
Cover designed by Ned Hoste, 2H

Typeset by Nick Hern Books, London
Printed in the UK by CLE Print Ltd, St Ives, Cambs, PE27 3LE

A CIP catalogue record for this book is available from the British Library

ISBN   978 1 84842 093 9